Contents

Overview		4
Level 2		6
Objective 1	Read sight words using time-delay instruction.	7
Objective 2	Point to sight words to complete sentences.	17
Objective 3	Point to text as it is read	47
Objective 4	Say and/or point to a word to complete a repeated story line	61
Objective 5	Respond to literal questions about a story.	87
Objective 6	Demonstrate understanding of syllable segmentation by clapping out syllables in words.	101
Objective 8	Identify letter-sound correspondences.	107
Objective 9	Point to and/or say the first/last sounds in words	113
Objective 10	Identify pictures that begin/end with given sounds	119
Objective 13	Point to pictures/words representing new vocabulary.	135
Level 3		149
Objective 1	Read sight words using time-delay instruction.	151
Objective 2	Point to sight words to complete sentences.	163
Objective 3	Point to text as it is read	201
Objective 4	Say and/or point to a word to complete a repeated story line	211
Objective 5	Respond to literal questions about a story.	237
Objective 6	Demonstrate understanding of syllable segmentation by clapping out syllables in words.	251
Objective 8	Identify letter-sound correspondences.	257
Objective 9	Point to and/or say the first/last sounds in words	263
Objective 10	Identify pictures that begin/end with given sounds	269
Objective 13	Point to pictures/words representing new vocabulary.	285

Overview

The **Level 2 or Level 3 Assessment** should be administered at the completion of Level 2 and Level 3. The assessment is used to determine when a student is ready to move on to the next level of the curriculum. Test items measure mastery of the objectives taught in each level of the **Early Literacy Skills Builder (ELSB)** curriculum.

Preparation

Preparing for the administration of the assessment is easy:

- Practice the script for administering the assessment items before administering the assessment. Specific instructions for administering each item of the assessment appear opposite the response page for the student.
- Prepare for the student's mode of response if different from traditional pointing or speaking, and decide if you will need to modify the directions to accommodate the response mode.
- Prepare a **Recording Form** for the level being assessed.
- For Level 2, Objective 2, have available the sight word flashcards: me, is, friend, and green; and for Level 3, Objective 2, have available the sight word flashcards: want, he, is, boy, and green.
- Use 2" × 2" Post-it® notes to cover the yellow highlighted words for Objective 4 in the level you are assessing.

Mode of Response and Modifications

Students with significant disabilities may need individualized modes of responding, such as pointing, grasping, or eye-gaze. It is important that the mode of responding is consistent for both assessment and instruction of skills. The ELSB curriculum and assessment can be delivered using any response mode that can be conceived of by modifying the materials and the directions. Materials can be modified by printing them from Disc 1. They can be enlarged, laminated, cut apart, and/or adhered to eye-gaze boards or augmentative or alternative communication (AAC) devices. If using AAC devices, the responses should be preprogrammed. It is also appropriate to modify the directions in the assessment, for example, changing **Point to** to **Give me, Look at,** or **Touch.**

Allowable Verbal Prompts

Verbal prompts can be given only once. The prompt can be given after 5 seconds without a response. The allowable verbal prompts are given following the item direction.

- Have the **All About Moe** easel book with the stories "Moe Is Not Happy" and "Moe Is Happy" available for assessment of Objective 5 in Level 2 and "Moe Wants a Pet" and "Moe Gets a Pet" in Level 3.

Recording Forms

Reproducible Recording Forms for noting the student's responses for Levels 2 and 3 are included in Appendix E of the ELSB Implementation Guide. They are also included on Disc 1 for convenient printing. Note that the Recording Form allows you to enter information over time. The student responses on initial administration are recorded on the form under the Test 1 column and under the appropriate column for subsequent administrations of the assessment.

Using the Assessment to Determine Mastery

Administer the assessment to determine an individual student's level of mastery. Administer the level test once the student has completed Lesson 5 for the level. For each objective, total the number of items that were correctly performed independently (without prompting) and transfer the total to the Assessment Summary on the cover of the Recording Form. Add the total for each objective for a total level score. Divide the number of items correct by the total number of possible correct items. Multiply by 100 to determine the percent of correct responses performed independently for the level.

The recommended percentage for mastery of a level is 75% or greater. This percentage can be revised depending on a given student's needs. Higher percentages correct indicate a greater level of mastery. If a student reaches the level of mastery, it is appropriate to advance the student to the next level of ELSB. If a student does not reach mastery, there are three options:

1. Repeat the level, perhaps going at a faster pace, but reviewing all of the objectives. Then, re-administer the assessment to redetermine mastery.

2. Reteach selected objectives for which the student had difficulty. Then re-administer the assessment.

3. Advance the student to the next level, but monitor the student's progress. Many of the skills spiral through the curriculum and are addressed again in upper levels. If a specific skill is preventing the student from progressing, it is possible to continue on through the curriculum while addressing the objective with extra instruction at other times of the day.

Refer to the ELSB Implementation Guide for additional information on working with students who do not achieve mastery.

Level 2

Objective 1

Read sight words using time-delay instruction

dog   **Moe**   **is**

Demonstration Directions

Say, **I will find a word. Like this, *Moe*.** Touch the word *Moe*. Say, **Now you try it. Find the word *Moe*.** Allow 5 seconds for the student to initiate a response. If no response or an incorrect response, encourage the student to respond. Say, **Like this,** and repeat touching the word *Moe* and directing the student to find it.

me friend

Administration Directions

Present the student page to the student. Then say, **Point to *me*.** Pause for 5 seconds, waiting for the student to initiate a response.

Allowable Verbal Prompt

Which one is *me*?

friend   is

Administration Directions

Present the student page to the student. Then say, **Point to *is*.** Pause for 5 seconds, waiting for the student to initiate a response.

Allowable Verbal Prompt

Which one says *is*?

boy   friend

Administration Directions

Present the student page to the student. Then say, **Point to** *friend.* Pause for 5 seconds, waiting for the student to initiate a response.

Allowable Verbal Prompt

Which one is *friend?*

Objective 2

Point to sight words to complete sentences

Moe is a green frog.

Demonstration Directions

Say, **Now I'm going to read words in a sentence. Listen.** Read the sentence, pointing to each word as you read. Turn the page.

Moe is a _____ frog.

Materials

Sight word flashcards: me, is, friend, green

Demonstration Directions

Say, **See, here is the sentence. It has a word missing. Which word goes here?** Read the sentence again, pointing to each word. Pause at the blank space, and then say the last word. Present the *green* flashcard and one of the sight word flashcards and say, **Point to the word that goes here.** Do not label the word choices. If no response or an incorrect response, encourage the student to respond by saying, **Like this,** and then point to *green,* the correct word. Say, ***Green* is the missing word. Moe is a green frog.** Repeat the request to find the missing word.

Show me the picture, please.

Administration Directions

Say, **Listen.** Read the sentence, pointing to each word as you read. Turn the page.

Show _____ the picture, please.

Materials

Sight word flashcards: me, is, friend

Administration Directions

Say, **Which word goes here?** Point to the blank space. **Listen.** Read the sentence and point to the words. Pause at the blank space, and then say the last words. Present a sight word flashcard and the *me* flashcard and say, **Point to the word that goes here.**

Allowable Verbal Prompt

Which one? _____ **or** *me?*

Give the ball

to me, please.

Administration Directions

Say, **Listen.** Read the sentence, pointing to each word as you read. Turn the page.

Give the ball to _____, please.

Materials

Sight word flashcards: me, is, friend

Administration Directions

Say, **Which word goes here?** Point to the blank space. **Listen.** Read the sentence and point to the words. Pause at the blank space, and then say the last word. Present a sight word flashcard and the *me* flashcard and say, **Point to the word that goes here.**

Allowable Verbal Prompt

Which one? *Me* or _____?

The book is on the table.

Administration Directions

Say, **Listen.** Read the sentence, pointing to each word as you read. Turn the page.

The book _____ on the table.

Materials

Sight word flashcards: me, is, friend

Administration Directions

Say, **Which word goes here?** Point to the blank space. **Listen.** Read the sentence and point to the words. Pause at the blank space, and then say the last words. Present a sight word flashcard and the *is* flashcard and say, **Point to the word that goes here.**

Allowable Verbal Prompt

Which one? *Is* **or _____?**

She is at school.

Administration Directions

Say, **Listen.** Read the sentence, pointing to each word as you read. Turn the page.

She _____ at school.

Materials

Sight word flashcards: me, is, friend

Administration Directions

Say, **Which word goes here?** Point to the blank space. **Listen.** Read the sentence and point to the words. Pause at the blank space, and then say the last words. Present a sight word flashcard and the *is* flashcard and say, **Point to the word that goes here.**

Allowable Verbal Prompt

Which one? _____ or *is*?

Monique is her friend.

Administration Directions

Say, **Listen.** Read the sentence, pointing to each word as you read. Turn the page.

Monique is her _____.

Materials

Sight word flashcards: me, is, friend

Administration Directions

Say, **Which word goes here?** Point to the blank space. **Listen.** Read the sentence and point to the words. Pause at the blank space. Present a sight word flashcard and the *friend* flashcard and say, **Point to the word that goes here.**

Allowable Verbal Prompt

Which one? *Friend* **or _____?**

Kevin has a new <u>friend</u>.

Administration Directions

Say, **Listen.** Read the sentence, pointing to each word as you read. Turn the page.

Kevin has a new _____.

Materials

Sight word flashcards: me, is, friend

Administration Directions

Say, **Which word goes here?** Point to the blank space. **Listen.** Read the sentence and point to the words. Pause at the blank space. Present a sight word flashcard and the *friend* flashcard and say, **Point to the word that goes here.**

Allowable Verbal Prompt

Which one? _____ or *friend?*

Objective 3

Point to text as it is read

Molly is a happy frog.

Demonstration Directions

Say, **See this sentence? I will point to the words as I read. Like this.** Read the line, dragging your finger along as you read each word. Say, **Now you try it. Point to the words as I read.** Provide a prompt by pointing to the first word. Allow 5 seconds for the student to initiate a response. If no response, encourage the student by saying, **Like this,** and repeat by reading and dragging your finger along as you read. Slow the rate of reading to accommodate students who physically move slower. For all Objective 3 items, count movement left-to-right as correct. Students do not need to touch word-for-word at this level.

Allowable Verbal Prompt

Point to all the words.

Moe is a green frog.

Moe is not happy every day.

Administration Directions

While the student is viewing the sentences, point to the first word and say, **Point to the words as I read.** Pause for 5 seconds to wait for the student to initiate a response. Slow the rate of reading to accommodate students who physically move slower.

Allowable Verbal Prompt

Point to all the words.

Moe jumps up and down,

up and down,

up and down saying,

Administration Directions

While the student is viewing the sentence, point to the first word and say, **Point to the words as I read.** Pause for 5 seconds to wait for the student to initiate a response. Slow the rate of reading to accommodate students who physically move slower.

Allowable Verbal Prompt

Point to all the words.

Moe has a friend named Molly.

Molly is a happy frog.

Moe is a happy frog.

Administration Directions

While the student is viewing the sentences, point to the first word and say, **Point to the words as I read.** Pause for 5 seconds to wait for the student to initiate a response. Slow the rate of reading to accommodate students who physically move slower.

Allowable Verbal Prompt

Point to all the words.

Moe is not sad today.

Moe is happy today because…

Molly came to play.

Administration Directions

While the student is viewing the sentences, point to the first word and say, **Point to the words as I read.** Pause for 5 seconds to wait for the student to initiate a response. Slow the rate of reading to accommodate students who physically move slower.

Allowable Verbal Prompt

Point to all the words.

Molly sings,

"I love you, and you love me.

We're as happy as frogs can be."

Administration Directions

While the student is viewing the sentence, point to the first word and say, **Point to the words as I read.** Pause for 5 seconds to wait for the student to initiate a response. Slow the rate of reading to accommodate students who physically move slower.

Allowable Verbal Prompt

Point to all the words.

Objective 4

Say and/or point to a word to complete a repeated story line

Moe is a green frog.

Moe is a green frog.

| green | chair |

Note: For this demonstration and items 15–19, cover the word highlighted in yellow on the student page with a Post-it® note. If the student is nonverbal, preprogram an AAC device to say the repeated word for the demonstration item and items 15–19. Have the AAC device accessible to the student before reading the sentences so you can see if the student is anticipating the hidden word.

Demonstration Directions

Say, **I'm going to read sentences and say a hidden word. Then I'll point to the word down here. Like this.** Read the sentences, pointing to the words. Say *green* as you uncover the hidden word. (If using an AAC device, hit the button each time you read the word *green*.) Then touch below the word *green* and say, **Here is the word *green*. You try it. Tell me the hidden word and find the word down here.** Replace the Post-it® note. Read the line with the hidden word again. If no response or an incorrect response, encourage the student by saying, **Like this.** Then repeat by covering the word again, touching below the word *green*, and directing the student to point to it and say it (or use the AAC device).

Moe jumps up and down,
Up and down, up and **down**.

| clock | down |

Administration Directions

Say, **I'm going to read these sentences. Tell me the hidden word and find the word down here.** Read each line, pointing to the words. Pause at the hidden word. Uncover the word as the student says (or uses the AAC device to say) the hidden word. Allow 5 seconds for the student to initiate saying the word and pointing to it before moving on to the next item.

Allowable Verbal Prompts

Tell me the hidden word or **Point to the hidden word.**

Give me the crown!

Give me the **crown**!

| crown | pencil |

Administration Directions

Say, **I'm going to read these sentences. Tell me the hidden word and find the word down here.** Read each line, pointing to the words. Pause at the hidden word. Uncover the word as the student says (or uses the AAC device to say) the hidden word. Allow 5 seconds for the student to initiate saying the word and pointing to it before moving on to the next item.

Allowable Verbal Prompts

Tell me the hidden word or **Point to the hidden word.**

Moe is a happy frog.

Moe is a happy **frog**.

| chair | frog |

Administration Directions

Say, **I'm going to read these sentences. Tell me the hidden word and find the word down here.** Read each line, pointing to the words. Pause at the hidden word. Uncover the word as the student says (or uses the AAC device to say) the hidden word. Allow 5 seconds for the student to initiate saying the word and pointing to it before moving on to the next item.

Allowable Verbal Prompts

Tell me the hidden word or **Point to the hidden word.**

Moe is not sad today.

Moe is happy **today**.

| today | arm |

Administration Directions

Say, **I'm going to read these sentences. Tell me the hidden word and find the word down here.** Read each line, pointing to the words. Pause at the hidden word. Uncover the word as the student says (or uses the AAC device to say) the hidden word. Allow 5 seconds for the student to initiate saying the word and pointing to it before moving on to the next item.

Allowable Verbal Prompts

Tell me the hidden word or **Point to the hidden word.**

Moe sings.

Moe **sings**.

| turtle | sings |

Administration Directions

Say, **I'm going to read a sentence. Tell me the hidden word and find the word down here.** Read each line, pointing to the words. Pause at the hidden word. Uncover the word as the student says (or uses the AAC device to say) the hidden word. Allow 5 seconds for the student to initiate saying the word and pointing to it before moving on to the next item.

Allowable Verbal Prompts

Tell me the hidden word or **Point to the hidden word.**

Moe is a ==green== frog.

| green | chair |

Note: This portion of Objective 4 provides picture representation of the word. For this demonstration and items 20–24, cover the word highlighted in yellow on the student page with a Post-it® note.

Demonstration Directions

Say, **I'm going to read this sentence and point to a picture of the hidden word down here. Like this.** Read the sentence, pointing to the words. Point to *green* as you uncover the hidden word. Point to the green square at the bottom of the page and say *green*. Say, **You try it.** Reread the sentence while pointing to the words. Say, **Point to *green*,** when you uncover the hidden word. If no response or an incorrect response, encourage the student by saying, **Like this,** and repeat pointing to the green square.

Up and down, up and ==down==.

| clock | down |

Administration Directions

Read the sentence while pointing to the words. Stop at the hidden word and uncover it. Say, **Point to** *down*. Allow 5 seconds for the student to initiate a response before moving to the next item. If the student selects the incorrect word before you finish reading the sentence, score as incorrect. Put your hand over the picture and say, **Wait until I am finished,** and repeat the direction. This prompt may be provided once.

Allowable Verbal Prompt

Point to *down*.

Give me the crown!

pencil | crown

Administration Directions

Read the sentence while pointing to the words. Stop at the hidden word and uncover it. Say, **Point to** *crown*. Allow 5 seconds for the student to initiate a response before moving to the next item. If the student selects the incorrect word before you finish reading the sentence, score as incorrect. Put your hand over the picture and say, **Wait until I am finished,** and repeat the direction. This prompt may be provided once.

Allowable Verbal Prompt

Point to *crown*.

Moe is a happy <mark>frog</mark>.

chair	frog

Administration Directions

Read the sentence while pointing to the words. Stop at the hidden word and uncover it. Say, **Point to** *frog*. Allow 5 seconds for the student to initiate a response before moving to the next item. If the student selects the incorrect word before you finish reading the sentence, score as incorrect. Put your hand over the picture and say, **Wait until I am finished,** and repeat the direction. This prompt may be provided once.

Allowable Verbal Prompt

Point to *frog*.

Moe is happy today.

today

arm

Administration Directions

Read the sentence while pointing to the words. Stop at the hidden word and uncover it. Say, **Point to** *today.* Allow 5 seconds for the student to initiate a response before moving to the next item. If the student selects the incorrect word before you finish reading the sentence, score as incorrect. Put your hand over the picture and say, **Wait until I am finished,** and repeat the direction. This prompt may be provided once.

Allowable Verbal Prompt

Point to *today.*

Molly sings.

| turtle | sings |

Administration Directions

Read the sentence while pointing to the words. Stop at the hidden word and uncover it. Say, **Point to** *sings.* Allow 5 seconds for the student to initiate a response before moving to the next item. If the student selects the incorrect word before you finish reading the sentence, score as incorrect. Put your hand over the picture and say, **Wait until I am finished,** and repeat the direction. This prompt may be provided once.

Allowable Verbal Prompt

Point to *sings.*

Objective 5

Respond to literal questions about a story

green frog

red bird

> **Note:** You will need the **All About Moe** easel book with the "Moe Is Not Happy" and "Moe Is Happy" stories for this objective.

Administration Directions

Display the "Moe Is Not Happy" story so the student can see it. While you read the story, drag your finger along below the words. Ask the question immediately after reading the line where the answer appears.

Who is Moe? (Line 1)

Allowable Verbal Prompts

Repeat the question or ask, **Which one? A green frog or a red bird?**

Where is my crown?

Where is my glove?

Administration Directions

Display the "Moe Is Not Happy" story so the student can see it. While you read the story, drag your finger along below the words. Ask the question immediately after reading the line where the answer appears.

What does Moe ask? (Line 7)

Allowable Verbal Prompts

Repeat the question or ask, **Which one? Where is my glove?** or **Where is my crown?**

reads

frowns

Administration Directions

Display the "Moe Is Not Happy" story so the student can see it. While you read the story, drag your finger along below the words. Ask the question immediately after reading the line where the answer appears.

What does Moe do? (Line 10)

Allowable Verbal Prompts

Repeat the question or ask, **Which one? Reads or frowns?**

Molly

bear

Administration Directions

Display the "Moe Is Happy" story so the student can see it. While you read the story, drag your finger along below the words. Ask the question immediately after reading the line where the answer appears.

Who came to play with Moe? (Line 6)

Allowable Verbal Prompts

Repeat the question or ask, **Which one? Molly or a bear?**

Moe

Marquis

Administration Directions

Display the "Moe Is Happy" story so the student can see it. While you read the story, drag your finger along below the words. Ask the question immediately after reading the line where the answer appears.

Who sings? (Line 7)

Allowable Verbal Prompts

Repeat the question or ask, **Which one? Moe or Marquis?**

birds

frogs

Administration Directions

Display the "Moe Is Happy" story so the student can see it. While you read the story, drag your finger along below the words. Ask the question immediately after reading the line where the answer appears.

Moe and Molly are as happy as what?
(Line 10)

Allowable Verbal Prompts

Repeat the question or ask, **Which ones? Birds or frogs?**

Objective 6

Demonstrate understanding of syllable segmentation by clapping out syllables in words

under

Demonstration Directions

Say, **Listen. I will say words slowly and clap out the syllables.** Say the word *under* slowly, dividing the syllables (1 second per syllable) and clapping for each syllable. (Other movements—such as tapping on the table, a head nod, or a finger movement—are also acceptable. Use the movement most accessible for the student.) Say, **Try it with me. Un...der** (clapping twice). If no response or an incorrect response, encourage the student to respond by saying, **Like this,** and repeat clapping while saying **un...der** a third time.

happy

jumping

Molly

hello

today

Administration Directions

Show the student page and say, **Your turn. Show me the syllables as I say the word.** Say each word slowly, dividing the syllables (1 second per syllable) and clapping for each syllable. (Other movements, such as tapping on the table, a head nod, or a finger movement, are also acceptable. Use the movement most accessible for the student.) Allow 5 seconds for the student to initiate a response before moving to the next item. If the student starts to clap before you are finished, say, **Wait until I am finished**, and repeat. Score as incorrect.

Allowable Verbal Prompt

Your turn. Show me the syllables.

Objective 8

Identify letter-sound correspondences

Objective 8: Demonstration

f

> **Note:** Remember to say the sound the letter makes when the sound is written within virgules. Do not add a vowel sound (e.g., /f/ not /fuh/). Stretch the sound when multiple letters appear.

Demonstration Directions

Say, **This letter says the sound /fff/. Touch the letter that makes the /fff/ sound.** After 5 seconds, if no response, say, **Like this.** Point to the letter. **Now you do it. Touch the letter that makes the /fff/ sound.**

m a s

Administration Directions

Say, **What letter says the /aaa/ sound? Touch the letter that makes the /aaa/ sound.** Allow 5 seconds for the student to initiate a response. If no response repeat, **Touch the letter that makes the /aaa/ sound.**

For the remaining letters, be certain to make the sound of the letter and not say the letter name.

What letter says the /mmm/ sound?
What letter says the /sss/ sound?

Allowable Verbal Prompt

What letter says the /__ / sound?

Objective 9

Point to and/or say the first/last sounds in words

☺ <u>f</u>at

Demonstration Directions

Say, **See the red smiley face? This word is /fff/ /aaa/ /t/.** Say the word *fat*, stretching out the sounds as you say it. **/fff/ is the first sound in *fat*.** Point to the *f* and say, **Now you try it. Point to the first sound in *fat*.** Allow 5 seconds for the student to initiate a response. If no response after 5 seconds or an incorrect response, encourage the student by saying, **Like this,** and then repeat the request.

☺ **a**t

☺ **a**m

☺ **a**s

☺ **s**at

☺ **s**am

☺ **m**an

☺ **m**at

Administration Directions

Point to the green smiley face and say, **This word is /aaa/ /t/.** Say the word *at*, stretching out the sounds as you say it. Pause for 5 seconds and wait for the student to initiate a response. **The first sound in *at* is /aaa/. Point to the first sound in *at*.** If no response after 5 seconds, say, **Point to the first sound in *at*.** Point to it. Allow 5 seconds for the student to initiate a response before moving on to the next item. Repeat for each word on the page.

- **This word is /aaa/ /mmm/. The first sound in *am* is /aaa/. Point to the first sound in *am*.**

- **This word is /aaa/ /zzz/. The first sound in *as* is /aaa/. Point to the first sound in *as*.**

- **This word is /sss/ /aaa/ /t/. The first sound in *sat* is /sss/. Point to the first sound in *sat*.**

- **This word is /sss/ /aaa/ /mmm/. The first sound in *sam* is /sss/. Point to the first sound in *sam*.**

- **This word is /mmm/ /aaa/ /nnn/. The first sound in *man* is /mmm/. Point to the first sound in *man*.**

- **This word is /mmm/ /aaa/ /t/. The first sound in *mat* is /mmm/. Point to the first sound in *mat*.**

Allowable Verbal Prompt

Point to the first sound in _____.

Objective 10

Identify pictures that begin/end with given sounds

Objective 10: Demonstration • 120

Demonstration Directions

Say and point to each picture—**dog, rain, man, fan**—emphasizing the beginning sound as you say it. Say, **Point to a picture that has /fff/ as its first sound. Show me a picture that starts with /fff/.** Wait for 5 seconds for the student to initiate a response. If no response after 5 seconds, say, **The first sound in *fan* is /fff/. Touch the picture of the fan.** Allow 5 seconds for the student to initiate a response. If no response or an incorrect response, say, **Listen, *fan* starts with /fff/.** Repeat the request.

Allowable Verbal Prompt

Which one starts with /fff/?

Objective 10: Item 46 • 122

Administration Directions

Say and point to each picture—**apple, sun, pail, monkey**—emphasizing the beginning sound as you say it. Say, **Point to a picture that has /aaa/ as its first sound. Show me a picture that starts with /aaa/.** Wait for 5 seconds for the student to initiate a response before moving on to the next item.

Allowable Verbal Prompt

Which one starts with /aaa/?

Objective 10: Item 47 • 124

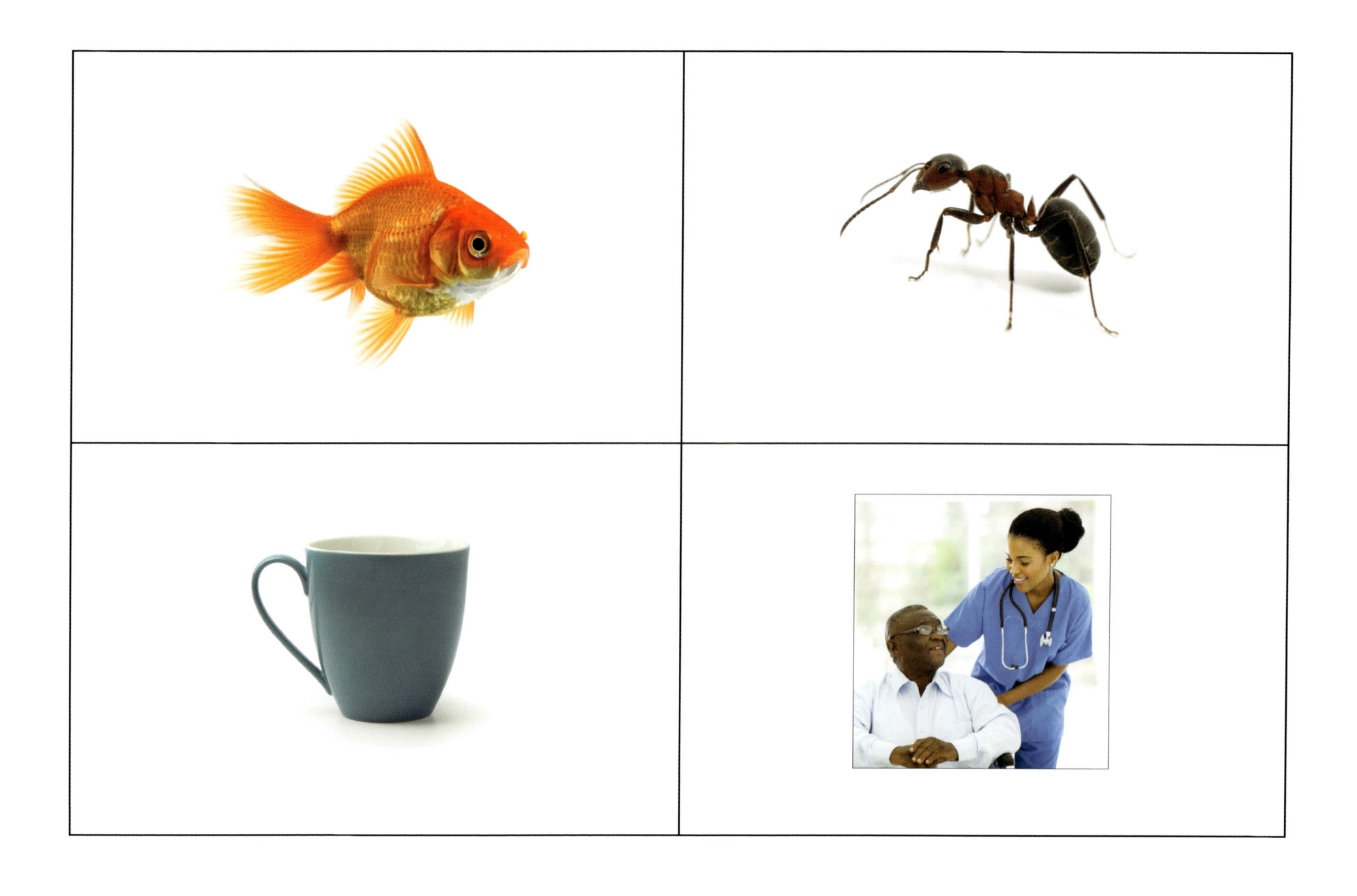

Administration Directions

Say and point to each picture—**fish, ant, cup, nurse**—emphasizing the beginning sound as you say it. Say, **Point to a picture that has /aaa/ as its first sound. Show me a picture that starts with /aaa/.** Wait for 5 seconds for the student to initiate a response before moving on to the next item.

Allowable Verbal Prompt

Which one starts with /aaa/?

Objective 10: Item 48 • 126

Administration Directions

Say and point to each picture—**mop, alligator, foot, saw**—emphasizing the beginning sound as you say it. Say, **Point to a picture that has /sss/ as its first sound. Show me a picture that starts with /sss/.** Wait for 5 seconds for the student to initiate a response before moving on to the next item.

Allowable Verbal Prompt

Which one starts with /sss/?

Objective 10: Item 49 • 128

Administration Directions

Say and point to each picture—**sun, nails, apple, tent**—emphasizing the beginning sound as you say it. Say, **Point to a picture that has /sss/ as its first sound. Show me a picture that starts with /sss/.** Wait for 5 seconds for the student to initiate a response before moving on to the next item.

Allowable Verbal Prompt

Which one starts with /sss/?

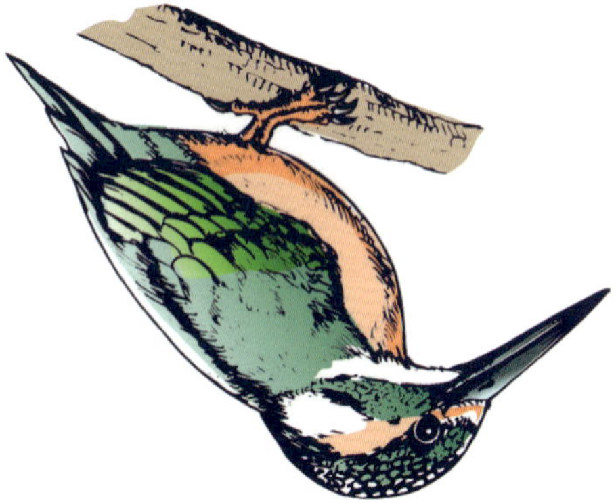

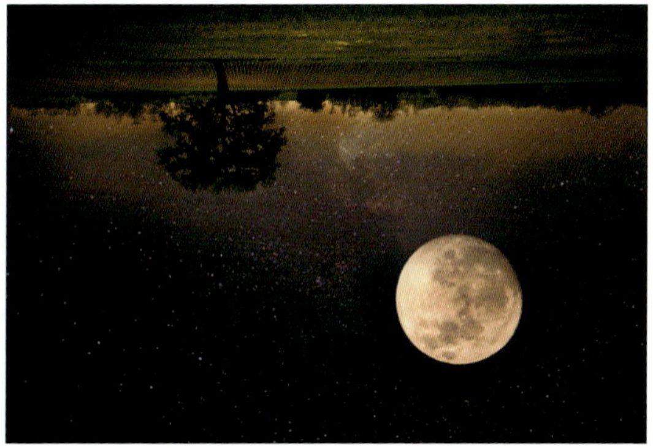

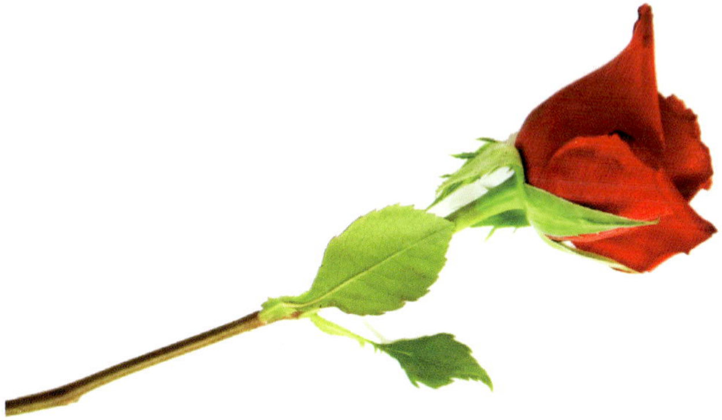

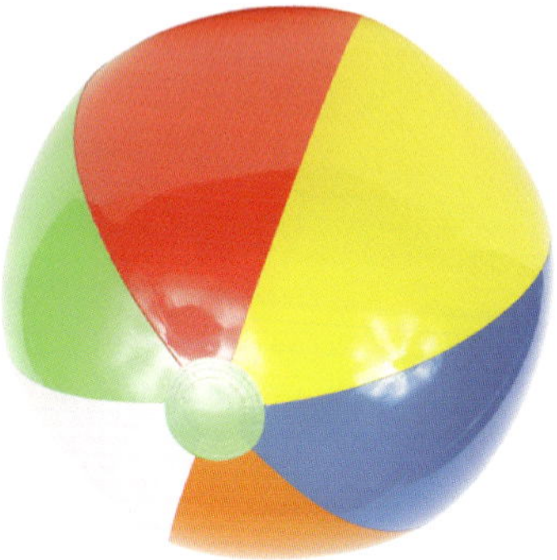

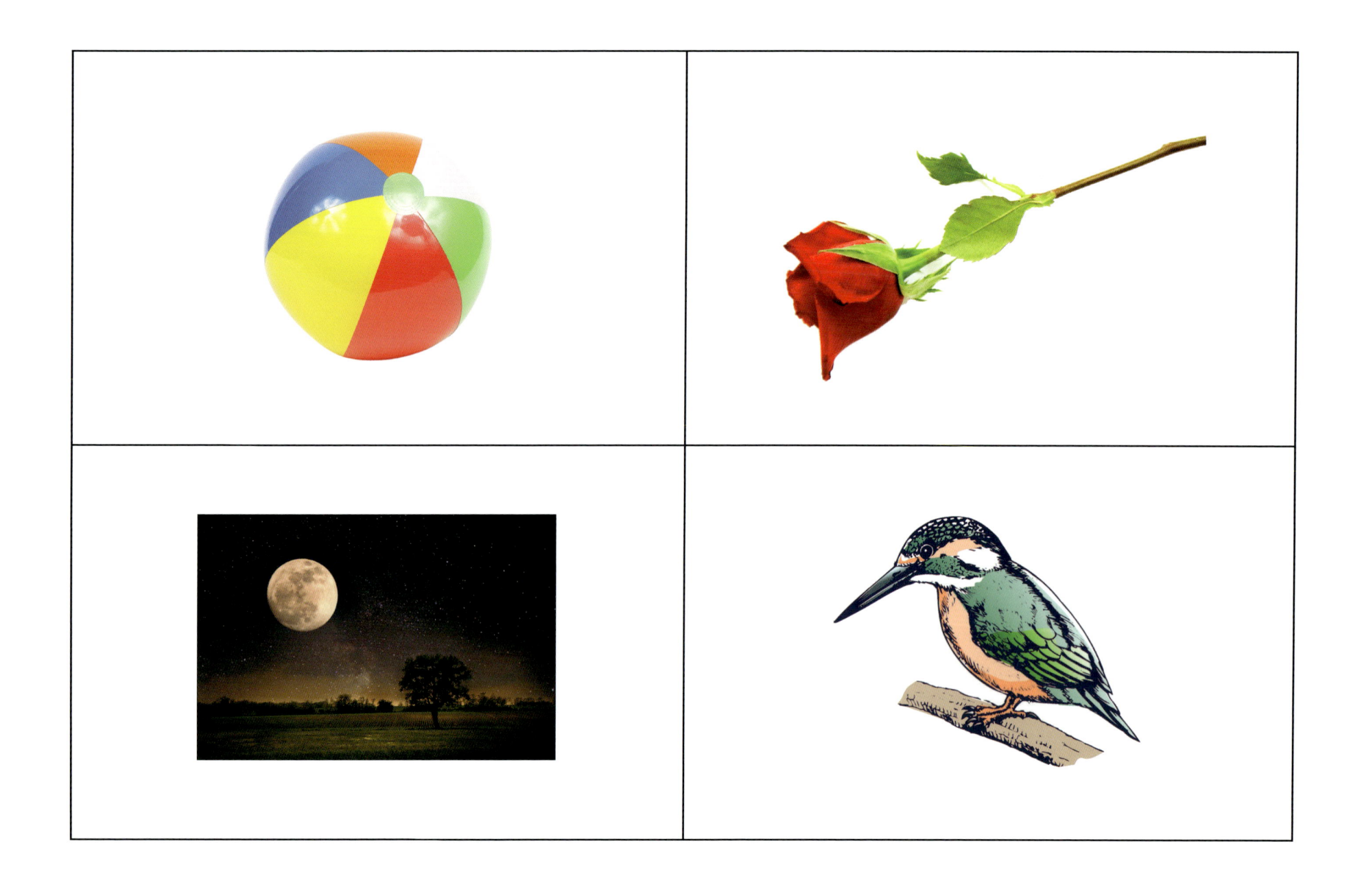

Administration Directions

Say and point to each picture—**ball, rose, moon, bird**—emphasizing the beginning sound as you say it. Say, **Point to a picture that has /mmm/ as its first sound. Show me a picture that starts with /mmm/.** Wait for 5 seconds for the student to initiate a response before moving on to the next item.

Allowable Verbal Prompt

Which one starts with /mmm/?

Objective 10: Item 51 • 132

Administration Directions

Say and point to each picture—**ant, sink, mouse, soup**—emphasizing the beginning sound as you say it. Say, **Point to a picture that has /mmm/ as its first sound. Show me a picture that starts with /mmm/.** Wait for 5 seconds for the student to initiate a response before moving on to the next item.

Allowable Verbal Prompt

Which one starts with /mmm/?

Objective 13

Point to pictures/words representing new vocabulary

bird	**sun**
tree	**sing**

Demonstration Directions

Say, **We are going to find some words, like *sing*.** Point to *sing* and pause for 5 seconds for student to initiate a response. If no response or an incorrect response, say, **This is *sing*. Now you point to *sing*.**

tree	bird
happy	socks

Administration Directions

Say, **Your turn. Point to *happy*.** Note: If the student selects the wrong word before you finish giving the direction, score it as incorrect. However, provide the student with an opportunity to learn to wait for the full direction. Prompt waiting behavior by putting your hand over the page and saying, **Wait until I am finished. Point to *happy*.**

Allowable Verbal Prompt

Point to *happy*.

apple

sad

bird

truck

Administration Directions

Say, **Your turn. Point to** *sad*. Note: If the student selects the wrong word before you finish giving the direction, score it as incorrect. However, provide the student with an opportunity to learn to wait for the full direction. Prompt waiting behavior by putting your hand over the page and saying, **Wait until I am finished. Point to** *sad*.

fan	**drum**
mad	**pot**

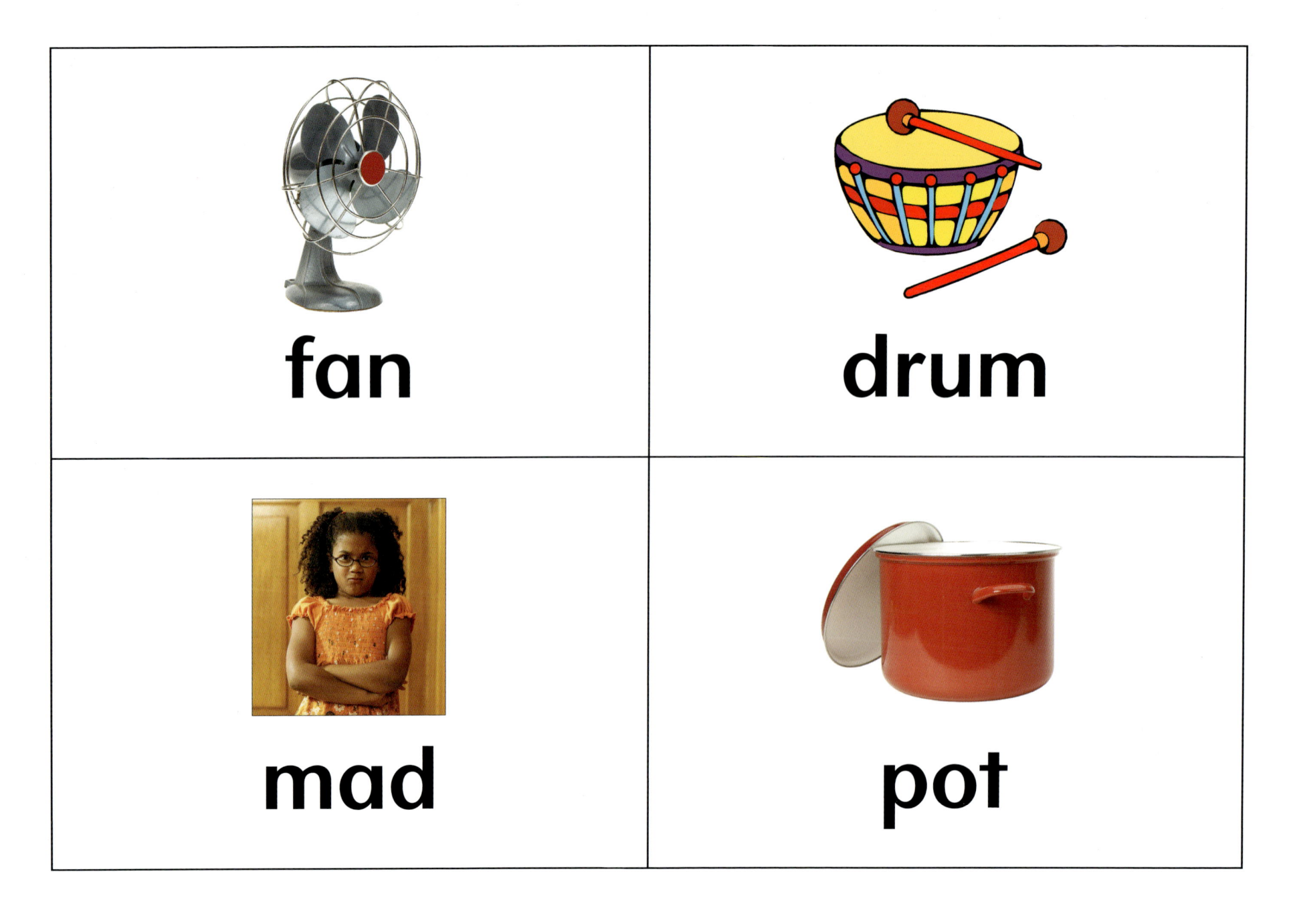

Administration Directions

Say, **Your turn. Point to** *mad*. Note: If the student selects the wrong word before you finish giving the direction, score it as incorrect. However, provide the student with an opportunity to learn to wait for the full direction. Prompt waiting behavior by putting your hand over the page and saying, **Wait until I am finished. Point to** *mad*.

Allowable Verbal Prompt

Point to *mad*.

scared	socks
dog	truck

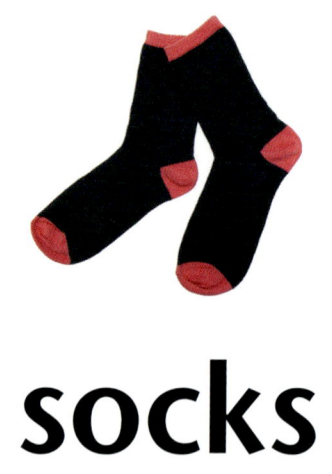

Administration Directions

Say, **Your turn. Point to** *scared.* Note: If the student selects the wrong word before you finish giving the direction, score it as incorrect. However, provide the student with an opportunity to learn to wait for the full direction. Prompt waiting behavior by putting your hand over the page and saying, **Wait until I am finished. Point to** *scared.*

Allowable Verbal Prompt

Point to *scared.*

fan	drum
pot	excited

Administration Directions

Say, **Your turn. Point to *excited*.** Note: If the student selects the wrong word before you finish giving the direction, score it as incorrect. However, provide the student with an opportunity to learn to wait for the full direction. Prompt waiting behavior by putting your hand over the page and saying, **Wait until I am finished. Point to *excited*.**

Allowable Verbal Prompt

Point to *excited*.

Level 3

Objective 1

Read sight words using time-delay instruction

dog   **Moe**   **is**

Demonstration Directions

Say, **I will find a word. Like this,** *Moe.* Touch the word *Moe.* Say, **Now you try it. Find the word** *Moe.* Allow 5 seconds for the student to initiate a response. If no response or an incorrect response, encourage the student to respond. Say, **Like this,** and repeat touching the word and directing the student to find it.

boy	want	friend

Administration Directions

Present the student page to the student. Then say, **Point to** *boy.* Pause for 5 seconds, waiting for the student to initiate a response.

Allowable Verbal Prompt

Which one is *boy*?

friend me want

Administration Directions

Present the student page to the student. Then say, **Point to *want*.** Pause for 5 seconds, waiting for the student to initiate a response.

Allowable Verbal Prompt

Which one says *want?*

boy girl he

Administration Directions

Present the student page to the student. Then say, **Point to *he*.** Pause for 5 seconds, waiting for the student to initiate a response.

Allowable Verbal Prompt

Which one is *he?*

is   friend   want

Administration Directions

Present the student page to the student. Then say, **Point to** *is.* Pause for 5 seconds, waiting for the student to initiate a response.

Allowable Verbal Prompt

Which one says *is?*

Objective 2

Point to sight words to complete sentences

Moe is a green frog.

Demonstration Directions

Say, **Now I'm going to read words in a sentence. Listen.** Read the sentence, pointing to each word as you read. Turn the page.

Moe is a _____ frog.

Materials

Sight word flashcards: want, he, is, boy, green

Demonstration Directions

Say, **See, here is the sentence. It has a word missing. Which word goes here?** Read the sentence again, pointing to each word. Pause at the blank space, and then say the last word. Present the *green* flashcard and one of the sight word flashcards and say, **Point to the word that goes here.** Do not label the word choices. If no response or an incorrect response, encourage the student to respond by saying, **Like this,** and then point to *green,* the correct word. Say, ***Green* is the missing word. Moe is a green frog.** Repeat the request to find the missing word.

I really <u>want</u> a dog.

Administration Directions

Say, **Listen.** Read the sentence, pointing to each word as you read. Turn the page.

I really _____ a dog.

Materials

Sight word flashcards: want, he, is, boy

Administration Directions

Say, **Which word goes here?** Point to the blank space. **Listen.** Read the sentence and point to the words. Pause at the blank space, and then say the last words. Present two sight word flashcards and the *want* flashcard and say, **Point to the word that goes here.**

Allowable Verbal Prompt

Which one? _____, _____, or *want?*

I <u>want</u> a cat.

Administration Directions

Say, **Listen.** Read the sentence, pointing to each word as you read. Turn the page.

I _____ a cat.

Materials

Sight word flashcards: want, he, is, boy

Administration Directions

Say, **Which word goes here?** Point to the blank space. **Listen.** Read the sentence and point to the words. Pause at the blank space, and then say the last words. Present two sight word flashcards and the *want* flashcard and say, **Point to the word that goes here.**

Allowable Verbal Prompt

Which one? *Want*, _____, or _____?

He is going to the pet store.

Administration Directions

Say, **Listen.** Read the sentence, pointing to each word as you read. Turn the page.

_____ is going to the pet store.

Materials

Sight word flashcards: want, he, is, boy

Administration Directions

Say, **Which word goes here?** Point to the blank space. **Listen.** Read the sentence and point to the words. Pause at the blank space, and then say the last words. Present two sight word flashcards and the *he* flashcard and say, **Point to the word that goes here.**

Allowable Verbal Prompt

Which one? _____, *he*, or _____?

First <u>he</u> saw a dog.

Administration Directions

Say, **Listen.** Read the sentence, pointing to each word as you read. Turn the page.

First _____ saw a dog.

Materials

Sight word flashcards: want, he, is, boy

Administration Directions

Say, **Which word goes here?** Point to the blank space. **Listen.** Read the sentence and point to the words. Pause at the blank space, and then say the last words. Present two sight word flashcards and the *he* flashcard and say, **Point to the word that goes here.**

Allowable Verbal Prompt

Which one? _____, _____, or *he?*

The rabbit is soft.

Administration Directions

Say, **Listen.** Read the sentence, pointing to each word as you read. Turn the page.

The rabbit _____ soft.

Materials

Sight word flashcards: want, he, is, boy

Administration Directions

Say, **Which word goes here?** Point to the blank space. **Listen.** Read the sentence and point to the words. Pause at the blank space, and then say the last word. Present two sight word flashcards and the *is* flashcard and say, **Point to the word that goes here.**

Allowable Verbal Prompt

Which one? *Is,* _____, or _____?

She is going

to the park.

Administration Directions

Say, **Listen.** Read the sentence, pointing to each word as you read. Turn the page.

She _____ going to the park.

Materials

Sight word flashcards: want, he, is, boy

Administration Directions

Say, **Which word goes here?** Point to the blank space. **Listen.** Read the sentence and point to the words. Pause at the blank space, and then say the last words. Present two sight word flashcards and the *is* flashcard and say, **Point to the word that goes here.**

Allowable Verbal Prompt

Which one? _____, _____ or *is?*

The **boy** found a turtle.

Administration Directions

Say, **Listen.** Read the sentence, pointing to each word as you read. Turn the page.

The _____ found a turtle.

Materials

Sight word flashcards: want, he, is, boy

Administration Directions

Say, **Which word goes here?** Point to the blank space. **Listen.** Read the sentence and point to the words. Pause at the blank space, and then say the last words. Present two sight word flashcards and the *boy* flashcard and say, **Point to the word that goes here.**

Allowable Verbal Prompt

Which one? _____, *boy,* or _____?

That boy can sing.

Administration Directions

Say, **Listen.** Read the sentence, pointing to each word as you read. Turn the page.

That _____ can sing.

Materials

Sight word flashcards: want, he, is, boy

Administration Directions

Say, **Which word goes here?** Point to the blank space. **Listen.** Read the sentence and point to the words. Pause at the blank space, and then say the last words. Present two sight word flashcards and the *boy* flashcard and say, **Point to the word that goes here.**

Allowable Verbal Prompt

Which one? _____, _____, or *boy?*

Objective 3

Point to text as it is read

Molly is a happy frog.

Demonstration Directions

Say, **See this sentence? I will point to the words as I read. Like this.** Read the lines, dragging your finger along as you read each word. Say, **Now you try it. Point to the words as I read.** Provide a prompt by pointing to the first word. Allow 5 seconds for the student to initiate a response. If no response, encourage the student by saying, **Like this,** and repeat by reading and dragging your finger along as you read. Slow the rate of reading to accommodate students who physically move slower. For all Objective 3 items, count movement left-to-right as correct. Students do not need to touch word-for-word at this level.

Allowable Verbal Prompt

Point to all the words.

Moe, the green frog, is excited!

He is going to the pet store

to get one pet.

Administration Directions

While the student is viewing the sentences, point to the first word and say, **Point to the words as I read.** Pause for 5 seconds to wait for the student to initiate a response. Slow the rate of reading to accommodate students who physically move slower.

Allowable Verbal Prompt

Point to all the words.

"I could get a rabbit," said Moe.

"But…I really want a dog.

Or I could get a cat."

Administration Directions

While the student is viewing the sentences, point to the first word and say, **Point to the words as I read.** Pause for 5 seconds to wait for the student to initiate a response. Slow the rate of reading to accommodate students who physically move slower.

Allowable Verbal Prompt

Point to all the words.

Moe went to the store to get a pet.

Moe still didn't know what pet he would get...yet!

First, he saw a dog sitting on a mat.

Moe said, "I like that dog."

Administration Directions

While the student is viewing the sentences, point to the first word and say, **Point to the words as I read.** Pause for 5 seconds to wait for the student to initiate a response. Slow the rate of reading to accommodate students who physically move slower.

Allowable Verbal Prompt

Point to all the words.

Objective 4

Say and/or point to a word to complete a repeated story line

Moe is a green frog.

Moe is a green frog.

| green | chair |

Note: For this demonstration and items 16–20, cover the word in orange on the student page with a Post-it® note. If the student is nonverbal, preprogram an AAC device to say the repeated word for the demonstration item and items 16–20. Have the AAC device accessible to the student before reading the sentences so you can see if the student is anticipating the hidden word.

Demonstration Directions

Say, **I'm going to read sentences and say a hidden word. Then I'll point to the word down here. Like this.** Read the sentences, pointing to the words. Say *green* as you uncover the hidden word. (If using an AAC device, hit the button each time you read the word *green*.) Then touch below the word *green* and say, **Here is the word *green*. You try it. Tell me the hidden word and find the word down here.** Replace the Post-it® note. Read the line with the hidden word again. If no response or an incorrect response, encourage the student by saying, **Like this.** Then repeat by covering the word again, touching below the word *green*, and directing the student to point to it and say it (or use the AAC device).

He is going to the pet store to get one pet.
But Moe doesn't know which pet he wants yet!

| bus | shirt | pet |

Administration Directions

Say, **I'm going to read these sentences. Tell me the hidden word and find the word down here.** Read each line, pointing to the words. Pause at the hidden word. Uncover the word as the student says (or uses the AAC device to say) the hidden word. Allow 5 seconds for the student to initiate saying the word and pointing to it before moving on to the next item.

Allowable Verbal Prompts

Tell me the hidden word or **Point to the hidden word.**

"But…I really want a dog.
I could get a bird.
But…I really want a **dog**!"

| pig | dog | cat |

Administration Directions

Say, **I'm going to read these sentences. Tell me the hidden word and find the word down here.** Read each line, pointing to the words. Pause at the hidden word. Uncover the word as the student says (or uses the AAC device to say) the hidden word. Allow 5 seconds for the student to initiate saying the word and pointing to it before moving on to the next item.

Allowable Verbal Prompts

Tell me the hidden word or **Point to the hidden word.**

First, he saw
a dog sitting on a mat.
Moe said, "I like that dog."

| dog | cat | pig |

Administration Directions

Say, **I'm going to read these sentences. Tell me the hidden word and find the word down here.** Read each line, pointing to the words. Pause at the hidden word. Uncover the word as the student says (or uses the AAC device to say) the hidden word. Allow 5 seconds for the student to initiate saying the word and pointing to it before moving on to the next item.

Allowable Verbal Prompts

Tell me the hidden word or **Point to the hidden word.**

Then, he saw a cat.
"I like that cat."

| snake | cat | goat |

Administration Directions

Say, **I'm going to read these sentences. Tell me the hidden word and find the word down here.** Read each line, pointing to the words. Pause at the hidden word. Uncover the word as the student says (or uses the AAC device to say) the hidden word. Allow 5 seconds for the student to initiate saying the word and pointing to it before moving on to the next item.

Allowable Verbal Prompts

Tell me the hidden word or **Point to the hidden word.**

But Moe could get only one pet.

"Yikes, I can get only one pet!"

| one | two | three |

Administration Directions

Say, **I'm going to read these sentences. Tell me the hidden word and find the word down here.** Read each line, pointing to the words. Pause at the hidden word. Uncover the word as the student says (or uses the AAC device to say) the hidden word. Allow 5 seconds for the student to initiate saying the word and pointing to it before moving on to the next item.

Allowable Verbal Prompts

Tell me the hidden word or **Point to the hidden word.**

Moe is a green frog.

green

chair

> **Note:** This portion of Objective 4 provides picture representation of the word. For this demonstration and items 21–25, cover the word in orange on the student page with a Post-it® note.

Demonstration Directions

Say, **I'm going to read this sentence and point to a picture of the hidden word down here. Like this.** Read the sentence, pointing to the words. Point to *green* as you uncover the hidden word. Point to the green square at the bottom of the page and say ***green.*** Say, **You try it.** Reread the sentence while pointing to the words. Say, **Point to *green*,** when you uncover the hidden word. If no response or an incorrect response, encourage the student by saying, **Like this**, and repeat pointing to the green square.

He is going to the pet store to get one pet.
But Moe doesn't know which pet he wants yet!

| coat | bus | pet |

Administration Directions

Read the sentences while pointing to the words. Stop at the hidden word and uncover it. Say, **Point to *pet*.** Allow 5 seconds for the student to initiate a response before moving on to the next item. If the student selects the incorrect word before you finish reading the sentence, score as incorrect. Put your hand over the picture and say, **Wait until I am finished,** and repeat the direction. This prompt may be provided once.

Allowable Verbal Prompt

Point to *pet*.

"But…I really want a dog!
I could get a bird.
But…I really want a dog!"

| pig | cat | dog |

Administration Directions

Read the sentences while pointing to the words. Stop at the hidden word and uncover it. Say, **Point to** *dog.* Allow 5 seconds for the student to initiate a response before moving on to the next item. If the student selects the incorrect word before you finish reading the sentence, score as incorrect. Put your hand over the picture and say, **Wait until I am finished,** and repeat the direction. This prompt may be provided once.

Allowable Verbal Prompt

Point to *dog.*

First, he saw a dog sitting on a mat.

Moe said, "I like that dog."

| cat | dog | pig |

Administration Directions

Read the sentences while pointing to the words. Stop at the hidden word and uncover it. Say, **Point to** *dog.* Allow 5 seconds for the student to initiate a response before moving on to the next item. If the student selects the incorrect word before you finish reading the sentence, score as incorrect. Put your hand over the picture and say, **Wait until I am finished,** and repeat the direction. This prompt may be provided once.

Allowable Verbal Prompt

Point to *dog.*

Then, he saw a cat!
"I like that cat."

| goat | snake | cat |

Administration Directions

Read the sentences while pointing to the words. Stop at the hidden word and uncover it. Say, **Point to** *cat.* Allow 5 seconds for the student to initiate a response before moving on to the next item. If the student selects the incorrect word before you finish reading the sentence, score as incorrect. Put your hand over the picture and say, **Wait until I am finished,** and repeat the direction. This prompt may be provided once.

Allowable Verbal Prompt

Point to *cat.*

But Moe could get only one pet!

"Yikes, I can get only one pet!"

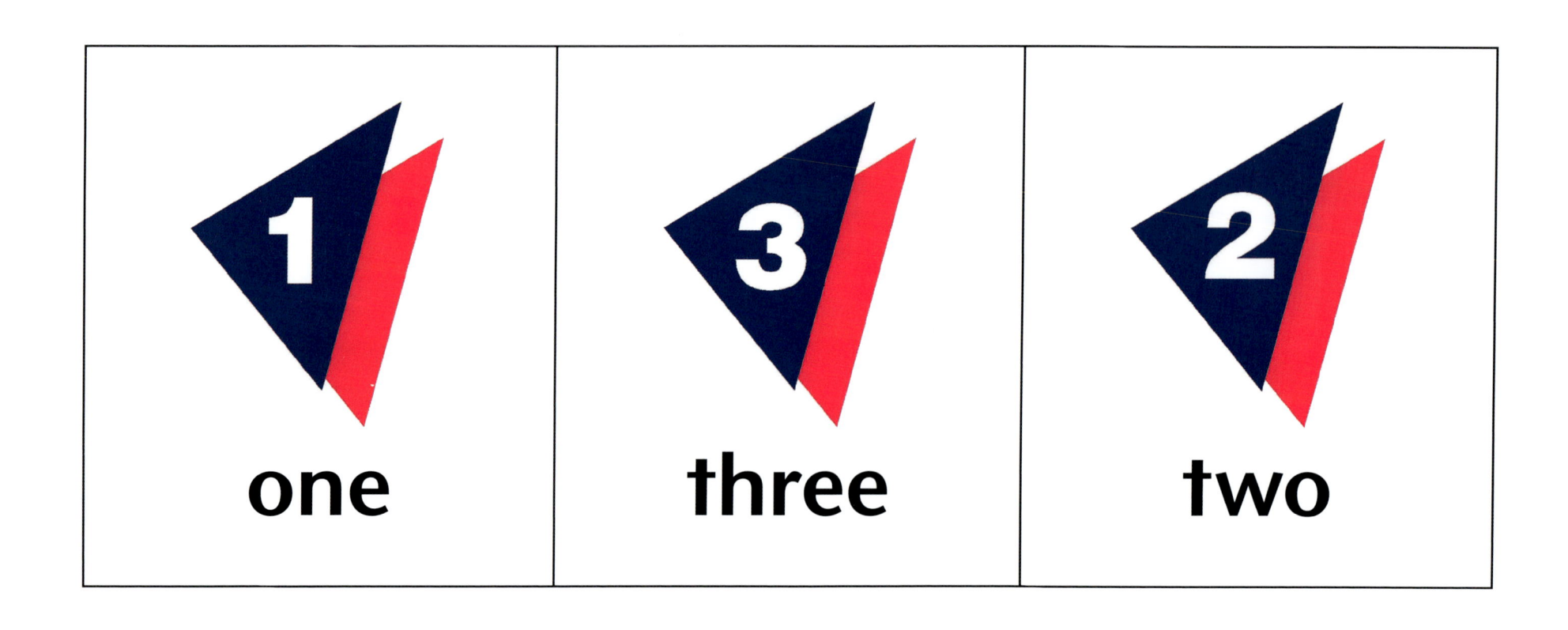

| one | three | two |

Administration Directions

Read the sentences while pointing to the words. Stop at the hidden word and uncover it. Say, **Point to** *one.* Allow 5 seconds for the student to initiate a response before moving on to the next item. If the student selects the incorrect word before you finish reading the sentence, score as incorrect. Put your hand over the picture and say, **Wait until I am finished,** and repeat the direction. This prompt may be provided once.

Allowable Verbal Prompt

Point to *one.*

Objective 5

Respond to literal questions about a story

grocery store | **park** | **pet store**

Note: You will need the **All About Moe** easel book with the "Moe Wants a Pet" and "Moe Gets a Pet" stories for this objective.

Administration Directions

Display the "Moe Wants a Pet" story so the student can see it. While you read the story, drag your finger along below the words. Ask the question immediately after reading the line where the answer appears.

What kind of store is Moe going to? (Line 2)

Allowable Verbal Prompts

Repeat the question or ask, **Which one?**
A grocery store, a park, or a pet store?

| one | three | two |

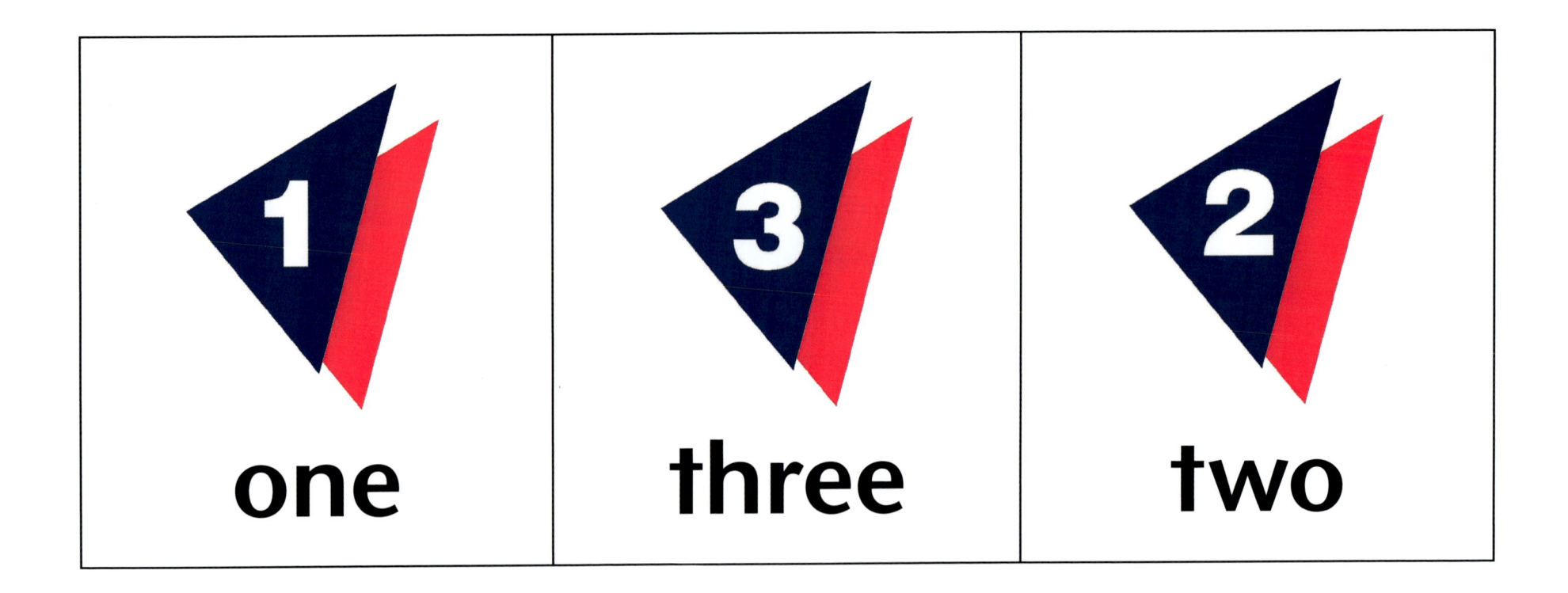

Administration Directions

Display the "Moe Wants a Pet" story so the student can see it. While you read the story, drag your finger along below the words. Ask the question immediately after reading the line where the answer appears.

How many pets can Moe get? (Line 2)

Allowable Verbal Prompts

Repeat the question or ask, **Which one? One, three, or two?**

dog | **goat** | **fish**

Administration Directions

Display the "Moe Wants a Pet" story so the student can see it. While you read the story, drag your finger along below the words. Ask the question immediately after reading the line where the answer appears.

What pet does Moe want? (Line 7)

Allowable Verbal Prompts

Repeat the question or ask, **Which one? A dog, a goat, or a fish?**

bird

dog

goat

Administration Directions

Display the "Moe Gets a Pet" story so the student can see it. While you read the story, drag your finger along below the words. Ask the question immediately after reading the line where the answer appears.

What did Moe see first? (Line 3)

Allowable Verbal Prompt

Repeat the question or ask, **Which one? A bird, a dog, or a goat?**

hat | **mat** | **bed**

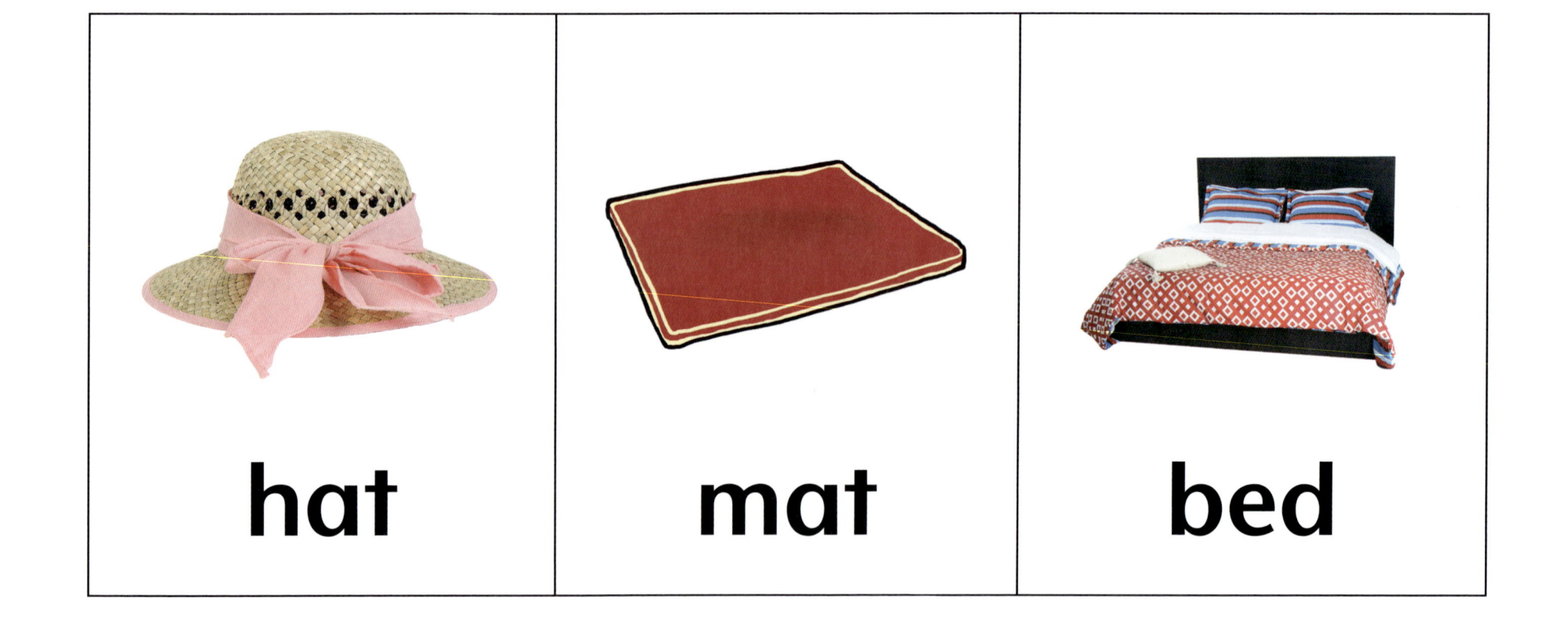

Administration Directions

Display the "Moe Gets a Pet" story so the student can see it. While you read the story, drag your finger along below the words. Ask the question immediately after reading the line where the answer appears.

What was the dog sitting on? (Line 3)

Allowable Verbal Prompt

Which one? A hat, a mat, or a bed?

bird

fish

dog

Administration Directions

Display the "Moe Gets a Pet" story so the student can see it. While you read the story, drag your finger along below the words. Ask the question immediately after reading the line where the answer appears.

What pet did Moe get? (Line 10)

Allowable Verbal Prompts

Repeat the question or ask, **Which one? A bird, a fish, or a dog?**

Objective 6

Demonstrate understanding of syllable segmentation by clapping out syllables in words

under

Demonstration Directions

Say, **Listen. I will say words slowly and clap out the syllables.** Say the word *under* slowly, dividing the syllables (1 second per syllable) and clapping for each syllable. (Note that other movements, such as tapping on the table, a head nod, or a finger movement, are also acceptable modes of demonstration. Use the movement most accessible for the student.) Say, **Try it with me.** *Un...der* (clapping twice). If no response or an incorrect response, encourage the student to respond by saying, **Like this,** and repeat clapping while saying *un...der* a third time.

Moe
jumping
hamburger
television

happy
pizza
excited
incredible

Administration Directions

Show the student page and say, **Your turn. Show me the syllables as I say the word.** Say each word slowly, dividing the syllables (1 second per syllable) and clapping for each syllable. (Other movements, such as tapping on the table, a head nod, or a finger movement, are also acceptable. Use the movement most accessible for the student.) Allow 5 seconds for the student to initiate a response before moving on to the next item. If the student starts to clap before you are finished, say, **Wait until I am finished,** and repeat. Score as incorrect.

Allowable Verbal Prompt

Your turn. Show me the syllables.

Objective 8

Identify letter-sound correspondences

f

Note: Remember to say the sound a letter makes when the sound is written within virgules. Do not add a vowel sound (e.g., /f/ not /fuh/). Stretch the sound when multiple letters appear.

Demonstration Directions

Say, **This letter says the sound /fff/. Touch the letter that makes the /fff/ sound.** After 5 seconds, if no response, say, **Like this. Point to the letter. Now you do it. Touch the letter that makes the /fff/ sound.**

t   s   a

m   r

Administration Directions

Say, **What letter says the /rrr/ sound? Touch the letter that makes the /rrr/ sound.** Allow 5 seconds for the student to initiate a response. If no response repeat, **Touch the letter that makes the /rrr/ sound.**

Note: Use the short vowel sound for /a/.

What letter says the /aaa/ sound?
What letter says the /t/ sound?
What letter says the /sss/ sound?
What letter says the /mmm/ sound?

Allowable Verbal Prompt

What letter says the /__ / sound?

Objective 9

Point to and/or say the first/last sounds in words

Objective 9: Demonstration • 264

☺ <u>f</u>at

Demonstration Directions

Say, **See the red smiley face? This word is /fff/ /aaa/ /t/.** Say the word *fat*, stretching out the sounds as you say it. **/fff/ is the first sound in *fat*.** Point to the *f* and say, **Now you try it. Point to the first sound in *fat*.** Allow 5 seconds for the student to initiate a response. If no response after 5 seconds or an incorrect response, encourage the student by saying, **Like this,** and then repeat the request.

☺ **r**at
☺ **m**at
☺ **s**at
☺ **t**am

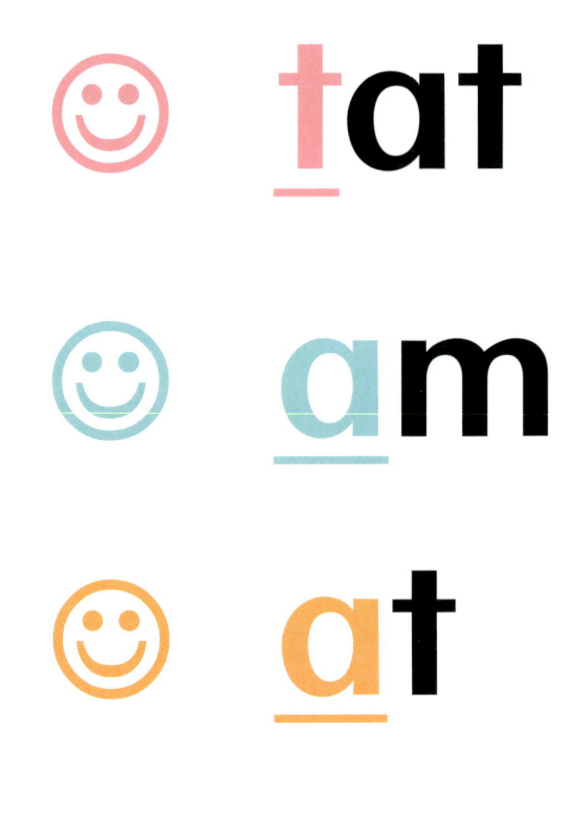

☺ **t**at
☺ **a**m
☺ **a**t

Administration Directions

Point to the green smiley face and say, **This word is /rrr/ /aaa/ /t/.** Say the word *rat*, stretching out the sounds as you say it. **The first sound in *rat* is /rrr/. Point to the first sound in *rat*.** Pause for 5 seconds and wait for the student to initiate a response. If no response after 5 seconds, say, **Point to the first sound in *rat*.** Point to it. Allow 5 seconds for the student to initiate a response before moving on to the next item. Repeat for each word on the page.

- **This word is /mmm/ /aaa/ /t/. The first sound in *mat* is /mmm/. Point to the first sound in *mat*.**
- **This word is /sss/ /aaa/ /t/. The first sound in *sat* is /sss/. Point to the first sound in *sat*.**
- **This word is /t/ /aaa/ /mmm/. The first sound in *tam* is /t/. Point to the first sound in *tam*.**
- **This word is /t/ /aaa/ /t/. The first sound in *tat* is /t/. Point to the first sound in *tat*.**
- **This word is /aaa/ /mmm/. The first sound in *am* is /aaa/. Point to the first sound in *am*.**
- **This word is /aaa/ /t/. The first sound in *at* is /aaa/. Point to the first sound in *at*.**

Allowable Verbal Prompt

Point to the first sound in _____.

Objective 10

Identify pictures that begin/end with given sounds

Objective 10: Demonstration

Demonstration Directions

Say and point to each picture—**dog, rain, man, fan**—emphasizing the beginning sound as you say it. Say, **Point to a picture that has /fff/ as its first sound. Show me a picture that starts with /fff/.** Wait for 5 seconds for the student to initiate a response. If no response after 5 seconds, say, **The first sound in *fan* is /fff/. Touch the picture of the fan.** Allow 5 seconds for the student to initiate a response. If no response or an incorrect response, say, **Listen, *fan* starts with /fff/.** Repeat the request.

Allowable Verbal Prompt

Which one starts with /fff/?

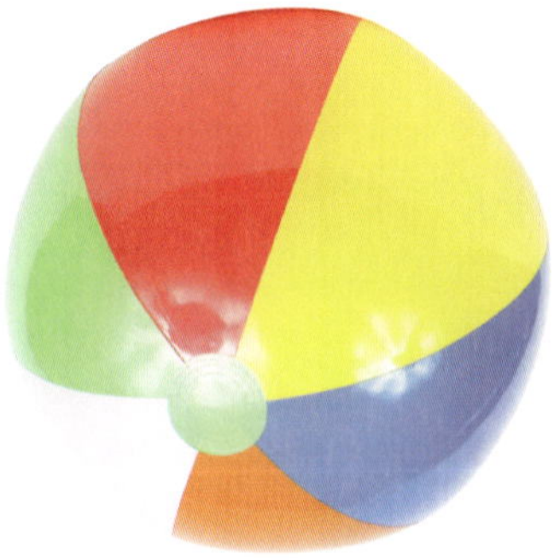

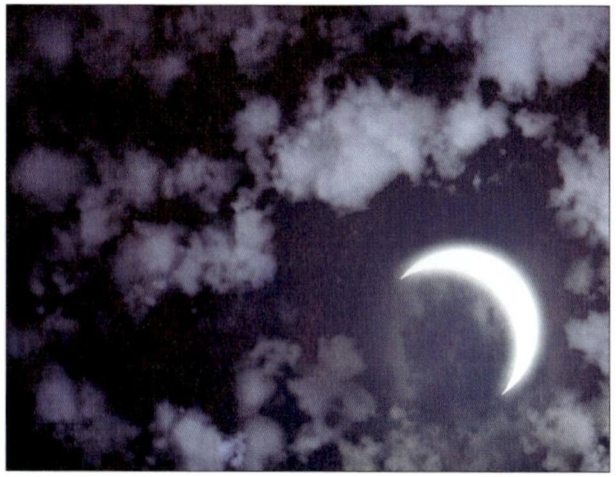

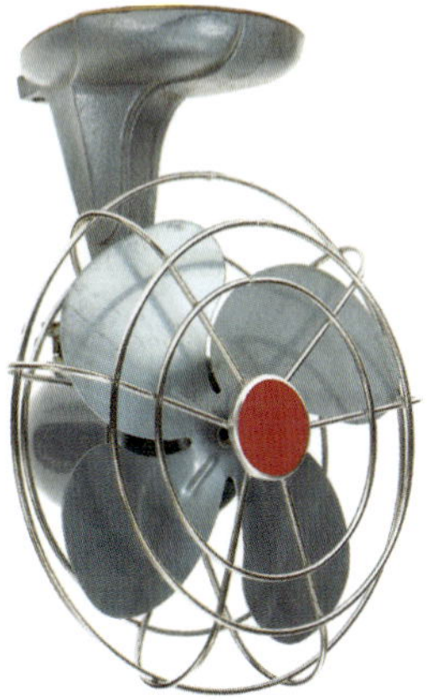

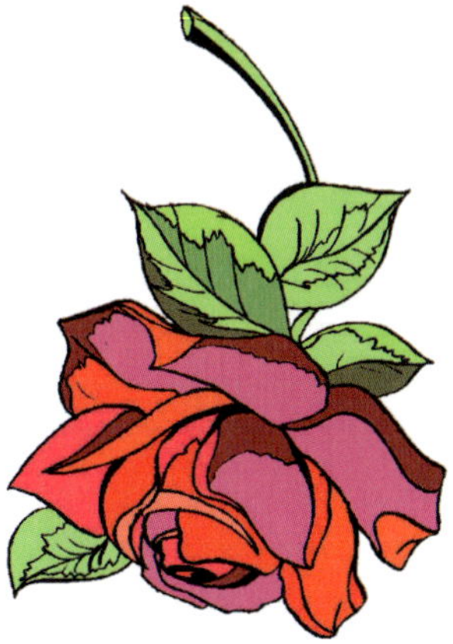

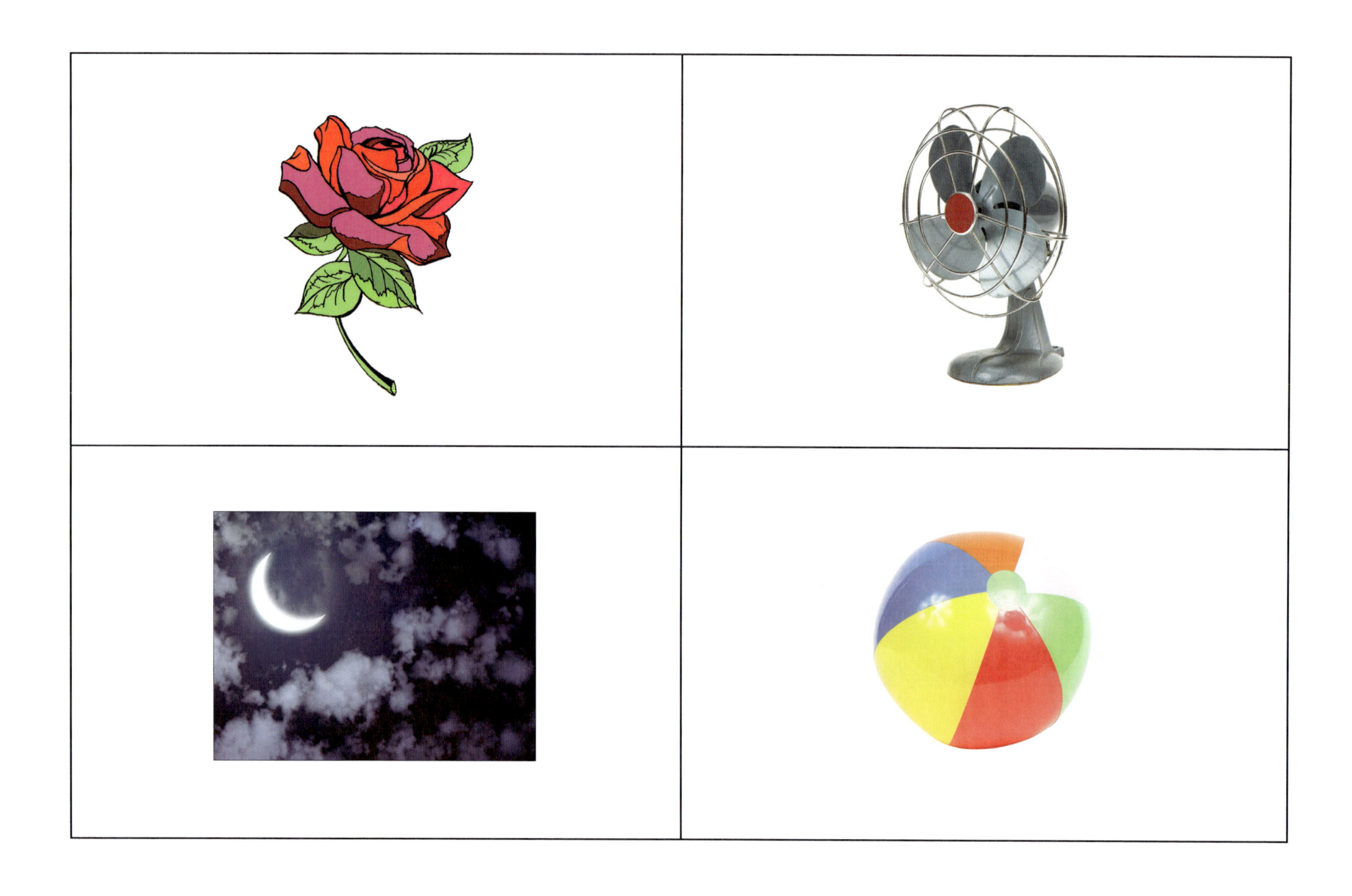

Administration Directions

Say and point to each picture—**rose, fan, moon, ball**—emphasizing the beginning sound as you say it. Say, **Point to a picture that has /rrr/ as its first sound. Show me a picture that starts with /rrr/.** Wait for 5 seconds for the student to initiate a response before moving on to the next item.

Allowable Verbal Prompt

Which one starts with /rrr/?

Objective 10: Item 53 • 274

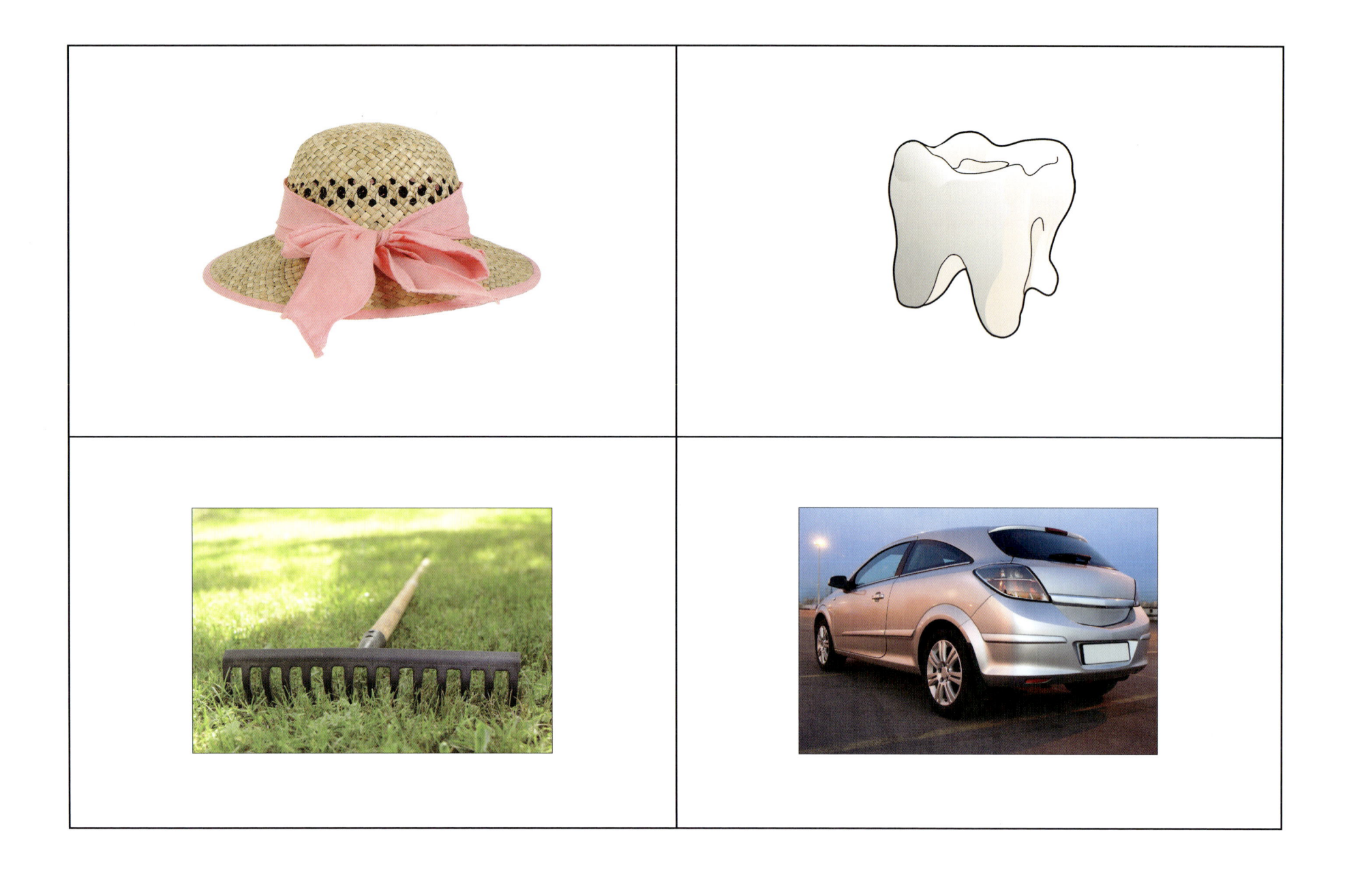

Administration Directions

Say and point to each picture—**hat, tooth, rake, car**—emphasizing the beginning sound as you say it. Say, **Point to a picture that has /rrr/ as its first sound. Show me a picture that starts with /rrr/.** Wait for 5 seconds for the student to initiate a response before moving on to the next item.

Allowable Verbal Prompt

Which one starts with /rrr/?

Objective 10: Item 54

Administration Directions

Say and point to each picture—**tire, fan, bug, soap**—emphasizing the beginning sound as you say it. Say, **Point to a picture that has /t/ as its first sound. Show me a picture that starts with /t/.** Wait for 5 seconds for the student to initiate a response before moving on to the next item.

Allowable Verbal Prompt

Which one starts with /t/?

Objective 10: Item 55

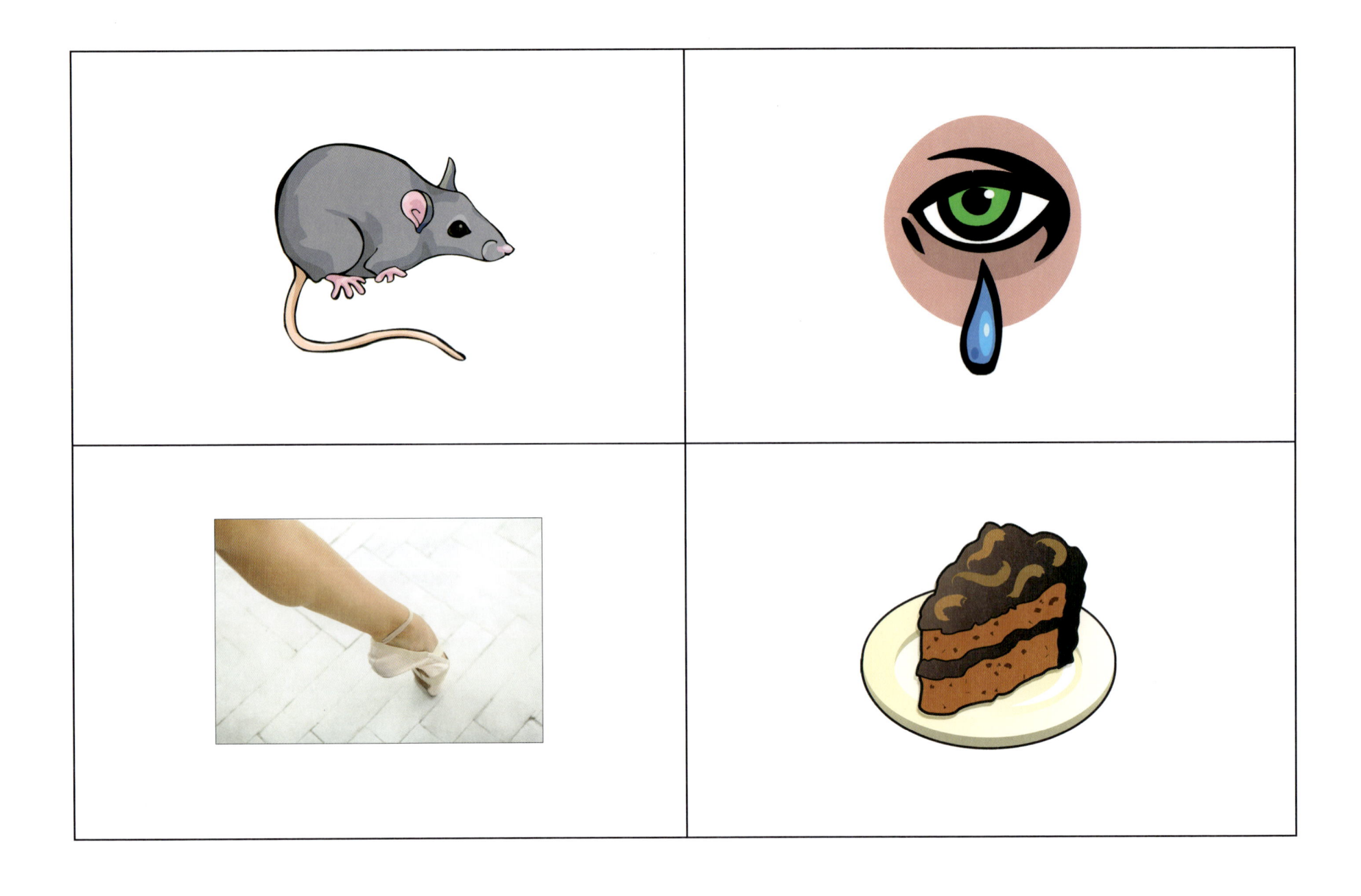

Administration Directions

Say and point to each picture—**rat, tear, leg, cake**—emphasizing the beginning sound as you say it. Say, **Point to a picture that has /t/ as its first sound. Show me a picture that starts with /t/.** Wait for 5 seconds for the student to initiate a response before moving on to the next item.

Allowable Verbal Prompt

Which one starts with /t/?

Objective 10: Item 56 • 280

Administration Directions

Say and point to each picture—**girl, apple, soap, fish**—emphasizing the beginning sound as you say it. Say, **Point to a picture that has /aaa/ as its first sound. Show me a picture that starts with /aaa/.** Wait for 5 seconds for the student to initiate a response before moving on to the next item.

Allowable Verbal Prompt

Which one starts with /aaa/?

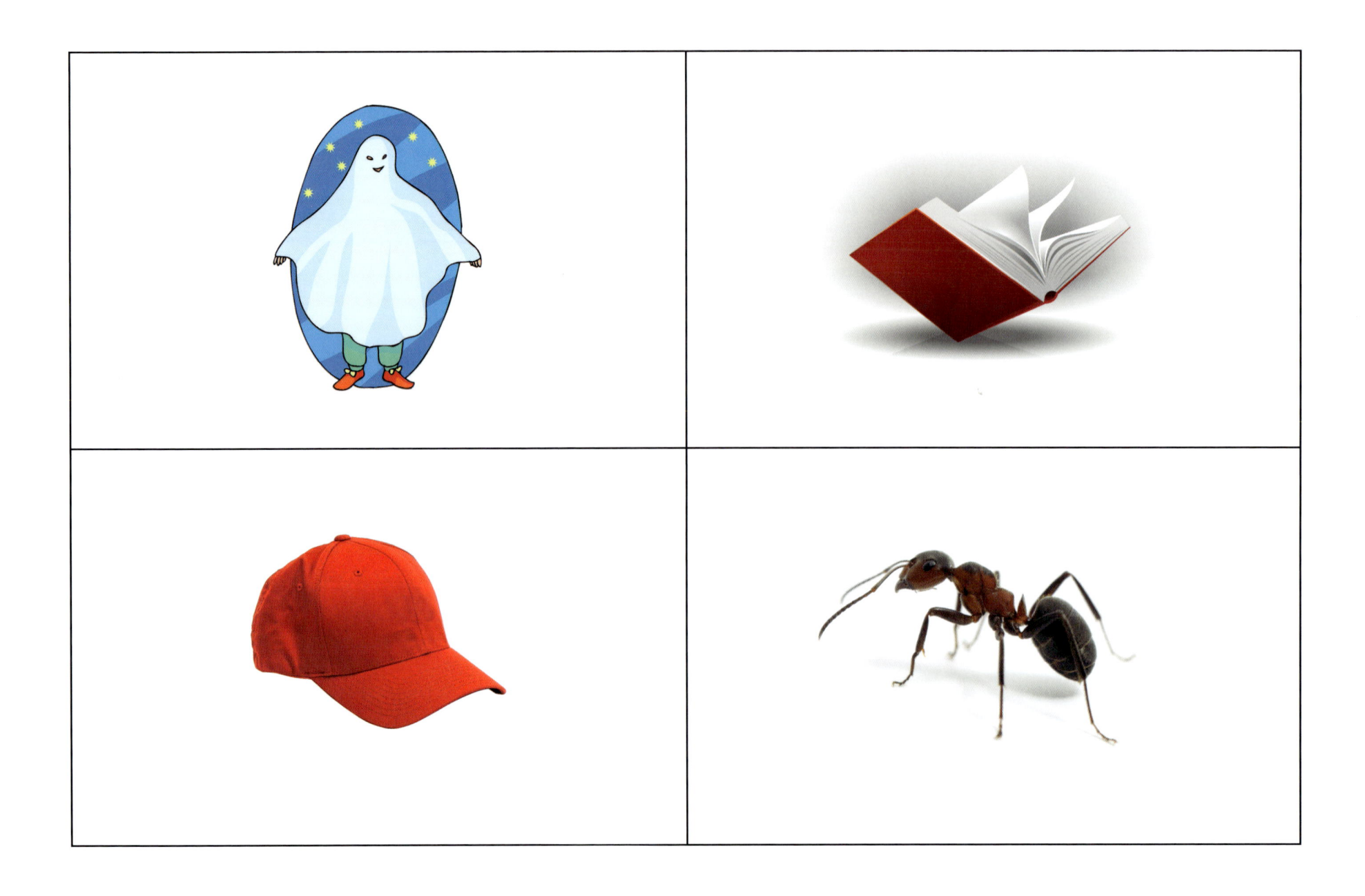

Objective 10: Item 57 • 282

Administration Directions

Say and point to each picture—**ghost, book, cap, ant**—emphasizing the beginning sound as you say it. Say, **Point to a picture that has /aaa/ as its first sound. Show me a picture that starts with /aaa/.** Wait for 5 seconds for the student to initiate a response before moving on to the next item.

Allowable Verbal Prompt

Which one starts with /aaa/?

Objective 13

Point to pictures/words representing new vocabulary

bird	**sun**
tree	**sing**

Demonstration Directions

Say, **We are going to find some words, like *sing*.** Point to *sing* and pause for 5 seconds for student to initiate a response. If no response or an incorrect response, say, **This is *sing*. Now you point to *sing*.**

socks

rabbit

man

dog

Administration Directions

Say, **Your turn. Point to *dog*.** Note: If the student selects the wrong word before you finish giving the direction, score it as incorrect. However, provide the student with an opportunity to learn to wait for the full direction. Prompt waiting behavior by putting your hand over the page and saying, **Wait until I am finished. Point to *dog*.**

Allowable Verbal Prompt

Point to *dog*.

pig

snake

fruit

ball

Administration Directions

Say, **Your turn. Point to** *snake.* Note: If the student selects the wrong word before you finish giving the direction, score it as incorrect. However, provide the student with an opportunity to learn to wait for the full direction. Prompt waiting behavior by putting your hand over the page and saying, **Wait until I am finished. Point to** *snake.*

Allowable Verbal Prompt

Point to *snake.*

giraffe	lollipop
cat	baseball

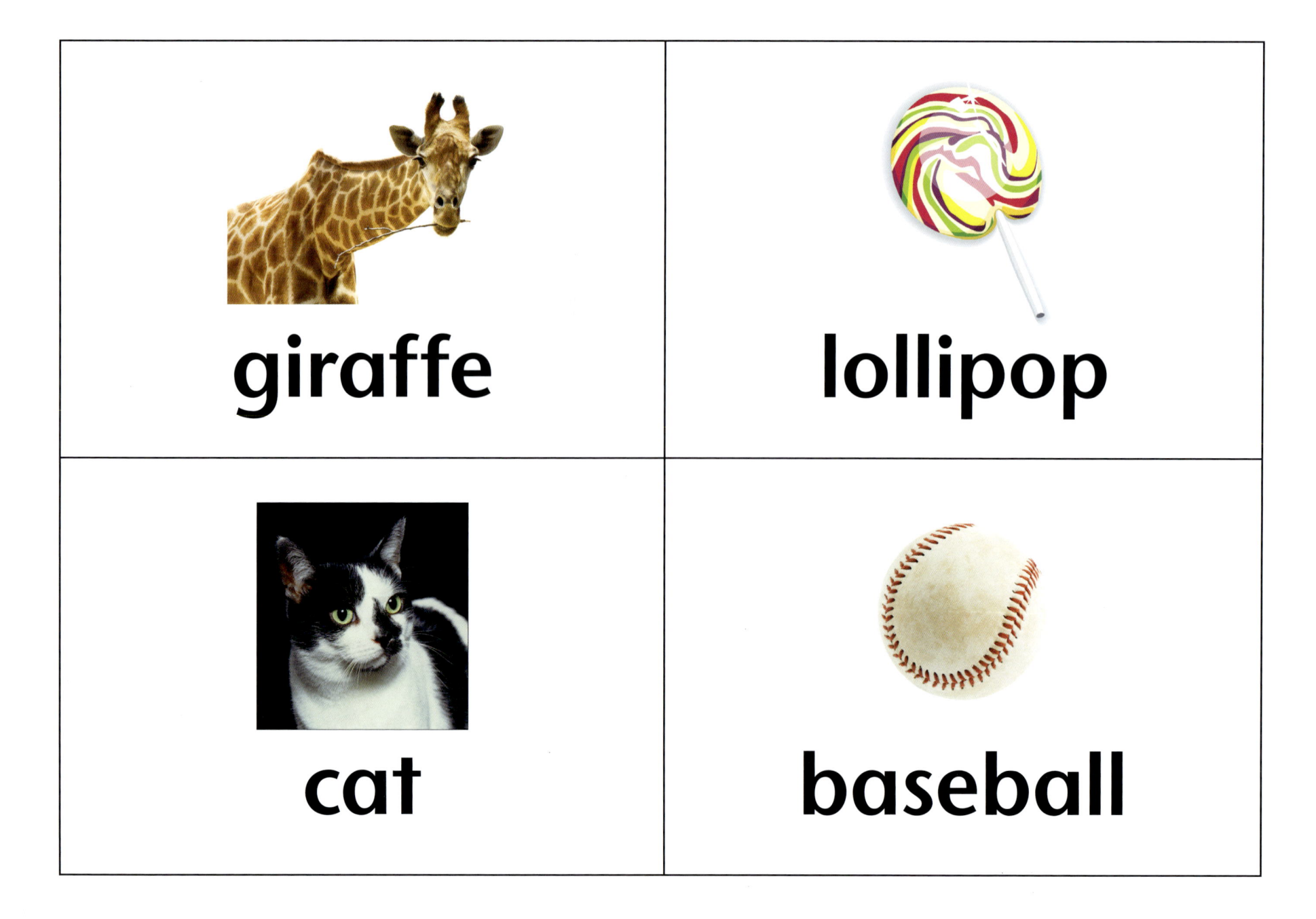

Administration Directions

Say, **Your turn. Point to** *cat.* Note: If the student selects the wrong word before you finish giving the direction, score it as incorrect. However, provide the student with an opportunity to learn to wait for the full direction. Prompt waiting behavior by putting your hand over the page and saying, **Wait until I am finished. Point to** *cat.*

Allowable Verbal Prompt

Point to *cat.*

giraffe	**fan**
ice-cream cone	**rabbit**

Administration Directions

Say, **Your turn. Point to** *rabbit.* Note: If the student selects the wrong word before you finish giving the direction, score it as incorrect. However, provide the student with an opportunity to learn to wait for the full direction. Prompt waiting behavior by putting your hand over the page and saying, **Wait until I am finished. Point to** *rabbit.*

Allowable Verbal Prompt

Point to *rabbit.*

bird	**cap**
tree	**trash can**

Administration Directions

Say, **Your turn. Point to** *bird.* Note: If the student selects the wrong word before you finish giving the direction, score it as incorrect. However, provide the student with an opportunity to learn to wait for the full direction. Prompt waiting behavior by putting your hand over the page and saying, **Wait until I am finished. Point to** *bird.*

Allowable Verbal Prompt

Point to *bird.*